The Truth About TV

Is It Television — or Hellevision?

by

EVANGELIST DAN GILBERT

This book has no price. A copy will be sent as a gift to everyone mailing in an offering of $1 or more to help sustain the Prisoners Bible Broadcast. If you wish the book, be sure to ask for it when mailing in the offering. Thank you.

order from
EVANGELIST DAN GILBERT
Upland, California

ISBN: 978-2-925369-49-3
Printed in the USA.

"Television is a greater menace to American youth than the atomic bomb, plus the H-bomb. The real hell-bomb, that shatters the soul as well as the body, is not carried by bombing planes. It is carried directly into millions of homes by the hellish influences that spread moral filth and corruption through the medium of television." — *Evangelist Dan Gilbert, in his special appeal for the outlawing of beer-drinking on television programs.*

Dr. Matthew N. Chappell, head of the department of psychology of Hofstra College, New York, made a full-scale scientific study of drinking among teen-age youngsters. He found that 90% of today's teen-agers drink alcoholic beverages. Girls drink as much as boys! "Junior and Junior Miss reach established patterns of social drinking at the age of 16!"

This is the "fruit" of the "television age" which turns the living room of the American home into a saloon. Teen-agers, at an alarming rate, are carrying into their own lives the pattern of beer-and-wine guzzling to be found on the TV screen.

IS IT TELEVISION — OR HELLEVISION?

Bible prophecy tells us all about television. It shall become world-wide. It shall be used by Anti-Christ to spread scenes of ugliness, wickedness, and crime before the eyes of people throughout the world.

In Revelation 11, we are told about the Anti-Christ "beast that ascendeth out of the bottomless pit." The Anti-Christ "beast" makes war against God's two faithful witnesses and puts them to death: "AND THEIR DEAD BODIES SHALL LIE IN THE STREET OF THE GREAT CITY, WHICH SPIRITUALLY IS CALLED SODOM AND EGYPT, WHERE ALSO OUR LORD WAS CRUCIFIED."

A Satanic spectacle is made of God's martyrs, murdered by the Anti-Christ beast. A world-wide television network is used to present this outrageous scene to all "kindreds and tongues and nations." Revelation 11:9: "AND THEY OF THE PEOPLE AND KINDRED AND TONGUES AND NATIONS SHALL SEE THEIR DEAD BODIES THREE DAYS AND AN HALF, AND SHALL NOT SUFFER THEIR DEAD BODIES TO BE PUT IN GRAVES."

We are fast approaching the time when this awful spectacle shall be enacted. It is estimated that 75,000,000 Americans already spend their evenings looking at television. And millions of more homes are "converted" each month into "receiving rooms" for all the filth, indecency, corruption, and ugliness that are spread before the eyes of mankind by means of television.

The mind and heart of humanity are being "conditioned" — that is, *hardened* — to look upon scenes of brutality and actually to *relish*, that is, *enjoy*, bloodshed and viciousness. Television serves the Devil's purpose of "schooling" and "educating" people in looking upon bloody violence as "entertainment." This will finally lead to the perpetration of the *Crime of all Crimes* — the murder of the Lord's two faithful witnesses, to be followed by the sadistic "viewing of the dead bodies" by television-corrupted "people and kindreds and tongues and nations."

Television is bringing bloody violence right into the living rooms of millions of Americans, who are being "educated" to "enjoy" entertainment, so-called, which consists of brutality and bestiality. *Time Magazine*, January 25, 1954, reports: "The toll mounted last week. One man was brained with a monkey wrench as he lay sleeping. A woman tied to a chair, was tortured with a carving knife until she died; two strip-teasers were sliced to death with razors; four gangsters were shot down in a columnist's living room; a bartender was murdered in his own saloon, and a small boy was killed by a drunken hit-and-run driver. A few victims survived, including the two teen-agers who were only beaten to a pulp, and the woman in the flimsy nightgown who was mauled by masked intruders in her bedroom, and the engraver who was shot through his working hand. All this slaughter and assault took place, respectively, on TV's *Rocky King, Dragnet, The Mask, Front Page Detective, Martin Kane, The Big Story, Big Town, The Man Behind the Badge,* and *Foreign Intrigue.*"

The United Press carries this dispatch from Sacramento, the capitol of the State of California: "Herman Stark, state director of the Youth Authority, said today that there is a marked increase in brutality in juvenile cases and he blamed television shows as one cause." He added, "the type of cases we are getting are a lot like the type you see on TV. There's a lot of this 'hit them over the head'. type of crime."

When a preacher points to television as a cause of youthful crime, there are always some people who will question whether or not he knows what he is talking about. Therefore, this preacher has dug up a mountain of evidence to support his own conclusions on this subject. Please listen to Dick Williams, who is "entertainment editor" of the Los Angeles Mirror. Naturally, Mr. Williams is in favor of television, movies, night clubs, and other dispensers of the pagan kind of "entertainment." But even this "entertainment editor" is fed up with the corruption of youth practiced by commercial exploiters of "television crime shows," as well as corrupt movies and indecent magazines.

Please consider what Mr. Williams has to say: "Public authorities are becoming increasingly alarmed at the current increase in crimes of violence—particularly among juveniles. The new outbreak of gang killings in Los Angeles, the recent senseless murder of the young insurance salesman here and the stomach-turning, fiendish kidnap-murder of the little Greenlease boy in Kansas City, point up anew that things are taking a turn for the worse. Why is this?

"My particular concern with this revolt against law, order and human decency is the part which popular entertainment mediums may be playing in it. I think it is considerable. Motion pictures, TV, comic books and true detective magazines are all helping to put heavy emphasis on the most lurid kind of crimes, their planning and their execution."

Mr. Williams goes on to tell of a currently popular "show," seen by millions in movie houses or on TV: "This is about a sex maniac who ravishes young girls, then cuts off their hair with large shears. It shows scenes of the killer lurking

behind a park bench in the bushes at late night to waylay a
pretty girl passing by. You see him pounce on her, drag her
out of sight and then hear her anguished screams as he
dispatches her. One of the final scenes shows an attempted
rape. What kind of entertainment is this?"

Well, what kind of *entertainment* is it? The kind that
appeals to the Devil himself. The kind "enjoyed" by the
fiends of hell.

Yet, this is the kind of entertainment being thrust into
the living rooms of millions of American homes each evening.
And it is the kind of entertainment, so-called, that millions
of American parents seem not to have the courage or char-
acter to *shut out of their homes.*

Yes, this the sad fact. Millions of church-going Americans
who have never visited saloons, brothels, or cheap movie-
houses are now permitting the saloon, the brothel, and the
sexy movie theater to come right into their living rooms and
corrupt their children.

A recent survey showed that 55% of the church people,
who used to listen to Gospel preaching every evening over
radio, are now spending their evenings looking at the filth
and corruption presented by way of TV.

It is true that there are some religious programs on some
television stations on Sundays. But I know of no television
station which carries an every-day religious program of any
kind. There are many radio stations that do. Yet, all the
surveys show that probably half of all church people, who
formerly listened to Gospel preaching every evening, are now
devoting their evenings to TV.

There are some radio stations that will not sell time to
the cigaret or beer companies. These are the stations that

carry my Prisoners Bible Broadcast each day. (XERF and KGER are two of them). These radio stations will not carry "crime dramas" or "sex plays" that cater to lust and degeneracy. BUT THERE IS NO TELEVISION STATION IN AMERICA THAT DOES NOT DEAL IN THE CORRUPTING ADVERTISING OF CIGARET AND BEER COMPANIES.

Some folks weakly protest, "but since there are religious programs on TV on Sundays, is it not all right to look at television?" Well, under this conception, your "looking" should be confined to Sundays!—since there are no every-night religious programs on television. But, please, understand this point. I am glad that the Gospel is presented on some television stations on Sundays. I am glad that the Salvation Army representatives go into saloons and distribute tracts. I am glad that I am able to go into jails and prisons and preach the Gospel of Christ. But merely because the Gospel is sometimes heard in saloons, in jails—or on television—this is no "argument" in favor of the patronizing of saloons, jails, or television by church people. I want to keep all church people away from jails, saloons—and television. But I know that sinners for whom Christ died are going to be found in saloons, in jails, and listening to television programs. Therefore, it is right and proper that we should do what we can to present the Gospel to people who are in jails, saloons, and listening to TV. But, at the same time, we should do all we can to encourage church people to stay away from saloons, obey the law and keep out of jail, and keep the saloon, the brothel, and the corrupt movie house from spreading filth in their living rooms by the medium of TV.

The magazine *Man's Life* has an article in the May issue

on the subject of how "FILTH IS BEING BEAMED STRAIGHT INTO OUR LIVING ROOMS BY TV." Art Rayburn, writer of the article, gives the proof that what he plainly calls SMUT is being spread by the cigaret and beer companies and others who are using television as a means of commercializing — making money out of — obscenity. In the beginning, the television industry was supposed to have a so-called "code of decency" of its own. But, since the biggest users of television have been the makers of beer and cigarets, the "television code" was about like the "saloonkeepers' code" — or the rattlesnakes' code. People in the saloon business have no decency, or they'd get out of that business. The television industry has no decency or it would not sell the largest part of its program time to the beer makers and the cigaret makers who are trying to increase their indecent profits at the expense of the health and morals of the American people.

From the beginning, the television business had no respect for decency. This was demonstrated by their shameful featuring of the "battle of the plunging necklines," with such "mistresses of undress" as Dagmar and Fay Emerson seeing who could come nearest to stripping themselves completely to the waist before the television cameras. Television has deliberately brought debauchery into the living rooms of millions of American homes, with displays of near-nudity that would result in arrests for indecent exposure on the streets of any American city where the law is being even half-way enforced.

In his article in *Man's Life*, Mr. Rayburn tells of the underhandedness by which some television stations pretend to have a "code of decency," while undercover they spread the worst kind of indecency. This is done by the device known as "ad lib." When a television performer does or says something "ad lib," the impression given is that it was not rehearsed, it was not known to the television station in advance. The indecency just "cropped" out, as if by accident. Therefore, no one is to blame! Of course, indecency *is* indecency. And whether obscenity appears on the TV screen, according to plan, or without plan, the effect upon the viewer is bound to be the same.

Mr. Rayburn says that some of the indecency seen and heard on television is planned and some of it derives from planless "ad libbing." However, if the television stations really wanted to get rid of filth, they would eliminate reckless "ad libbing." So long as performers are turned loose to say or do anything indecent that appeals to them at the moment, the defilement of the American living room will continue. So long as this irresponsibility continues, with no check put upon immoral "ad libbing," conscientious parents can follow just one course: have no traffic with TV.

Mr. Rayburn tells of a "little episode which took place on a performance of 'Break the Bank.'" A husband and wife got into some kind of argument — supposedly "unrehearsed" — which came to a climax "as she hissed: 'You stupid son-of-a—————.'" Mr. Rayburn comments, "She finished the word," for millions of televiewers, including many boys and girls, to hear.

One housewife later wrote, "Never had such language been heard in our home. My husband and I dedicated this home to Jesus Christ, and we have always tried to say only what He would have us to say. I feel that our home was made dirty and vile by what came in over the television receiver that night. We have purged our home, as best we could, by throwing out the television set. We are not taking any chances on the language of evil assailing us, unexpectedly, again."

She took the only course that a Christian homemaker can take, conscientiously and intelligently. The promoters of these "television shows" openly say that they cannot control "ad libbing," so televiewers never know when they are going to be assailed with new outbursts of obscenity and profanity.

Mr. Rayburn gives a number of examples of unspeakable foulness which has been "beamed" into millions of American living rooms by way of TV. The details are unbelievably vile. In one case, a performer deliberately acted in such a suggestive way as to cause other "panel members" to make hints and insinuations that the "performer" was engaging in a veiled form of masturbation — right there before the television cameras!

A favorite kind of television "humor" is built around the repulsive theme of "homosexuality." TV "performers" consider themselves at their "funniest" when they go through the mimicry of sex degeneracy.

Another TV specialty is the "dirty joke with the double-meaning." Such "humor" used to be confined to the brothel, the saloon, and the gutter. Now it is popularized as TV's form of "entertainment for the whole family."

Arthur Godfrey is supposed to be the master of the "double-meaning joke," which he tells with one foot in the gutter and his leering face in your living room, via TV. Let the expert investigator, Art Rayburn, tell you about Godfrey, the supposed idol of millions of TV fans: "Godfrey uses his 'heh heh heh' the way the average Joe says 'D'ya get it, Mac? D'ya get it?' after telling a not very funny off-color joke. I can recall Godfrey making all sorts of remarks about how Julius La Rosa got a sore lip; about the carloads of onions some admirers in Michigan were sending him 'And they keep sending telegrams suggesting what I can do with them . . . heh heh heh.' And the drooling leer, plus remarks to go with the leer, with which he sizes up the good looking gals who sometimes get onto his show."

While Arthur Godfrey deals in gutter jokes, the almost-as-popular TV star, so-called, Jackie Gleason paws over the young, good-looking girls in a way that would cause him to be arrested in any respectable hotel lobby in the land. Why, then, should he do it in *your* living room? It is within your power to rule him and all the other TV dirtiness out of your home. Mr. Rayburn has this to say about sex-offensive Gleason, "Lewd types of love-making still go on in spite of the TV Code's edicts, and you have only to look at Gleason in action or some of the avuncular comics who get the chance to kiss a sexy young gal to see what I mean. In some of the live dramas which go in for realism (a term which can be loosely defined as how-dirty-can-you-get?), you will see the same slobbering kisses and the tempestuous love-making that was outlawed for movies in the early 1930's."

The conclusion is: TV is even worse than the movies. We all know how vile the movies are. Yet, thousands of Christian parents who conscientiously keep their children away from the movies are permitting even fouler filth to come into their homes by means of TV. Serious thought, and Christian action, are certainly dictated on this subject, so far as many Christian parents are concerned. The simple truth is that the very lowest kind of filth, which finally was banned from the movies, has been dug up and dished out to the American people via

TV. Before more multitudes of American boys and girls are ruined, parents should wake up and recognize how television has been converted into the Devil's own instrument for piping rottenness into the American home. Given an opportunity, television will turn your living room into a combined brothel and saloon.

In his article, Mr. Rayburn gives examples of TV vileness that I cannot bring myself to reprint in this book. However, the evidence is clear and conclusive. The lowest filth on earth, the vilest corruption this side of hell, has been shoveled into millions of American homes by way of television. If anyone needs the convincing evidence, he will find it in this article, which gives names, dates, situations, and circumstances.

It has become a standing joke in the television business that Arthur Godfrey, celebrated as the biggest of TV stars, is a specialist in dealing in dirt. Mr. Rayburn reports, "When Fred Allen was told in the early days of TV that Godfrey's popularity was sweeping the country, he said: 'Godfrey *should* sweep the country and he should use a short-handled broom — he's so close to the dirt.'"

Shortly after this crack by Fred Allen, which nevertheless is a truthful description of TV star Godfrey, Mr. Rayburn reports that Arthur Godfrey, "almost died laughing when he showed his TV audience a picture of his own head superimposed on the figure of a girl in a brassier ad."

Do you want *that* going on in *your* living room?

Mr. Rayburn gives this description of what amounts to the projection of the brothel into the living room: "Women appear on TV with their bosoms busting out all over and their necklines down almost to their navels, and when they make love in dramatic scenes they behave like cattle in heat and kiss with a fervor that leaves everyone, including themselves, open-mouthed."

Such enactments of unbridled lust have been going on since the serpent entered into the Garden of Eden. In all past times, decent parents have kept their children away from places where such indecency was on display. But, now, millions of decent parents permit this kind of debauchery to come into the living rooms of their homes. When will Christian parents wake up, and cast out this leprosy of immorality that television is projecting into homes throughout our land?

I have given some space to Arthur Godfrey, because he is reputed to be among the two or three TV stars who have the largest witnessing audience. His vulgarity has become so obnoxious that professional "defenders" have rushed to his aid. One of them is Jack Mitchell who offers a "vindication" of Godfrey in the magazine *Top Secret, Hollywood, TV, Cafe Society, International*. Although he deals in gutter vulgarity, Arthur Godfrey makes a big pretense of being "religious"— in his own vulgar way, of course. In championing Godfrey, Jack Mitchell comments, "Godfrey can sound blasphemous even in prayer, like the way he exclaims: 'O hell, how I love God.' "

We should all pray for this poor misguided man. We should also pray for the millions of TV "fans" who idolize this misled "comedian" who calls it "prayer" when he bursts forth with his oft-repeated blasphemy: "O hell, how I love God."

While calling this awful blasphemy "prayer" in his own ignorant way, Arthur Godfrey twists the Scripture in the cheapest and most vulgar way to try to make money for his "sponsor."

Time magazine quotes him as follows (May 24, 1954 issue): "When it comes to chicken in Lipton's soup, you've got to have faith," Godfrey was saying. "Just like it says in the Bible. You know — the Book of Hebrews, Chapter 11, Verse one: 'Faith is the substance of things hoped for, the evidence of things not seen' (laughter—as reported in *Time* magazine). Or as it says in the Book of John, Chapter 20, Verse 29: 'Blessed are they that have not seen and yet have believed.' But don't go lookin' in the soup. It's there, but you'll never see it (laughter—as reported in *Time* magazine)."

Observing this unspeakable blasphemy on TV, Mr. William Ackerman of Chicago sent telegrams to both Godfrey and Lipton's tea company, complaining: 'Shameful, sacrilegious . . . intolerably obnoxious . . . loose disrespect . . . one of the lowest notes in television history."

From the tea company, Mr. Ackerman got this reply: "Like you, we were completely surprised at his reference to Scriptures. An entirely different commercial message had been prepared for him in connection with our product. Therefore, Mr. Godfrey's action . . . was without any prior knowledge or approval on our part . . . and we have already taken this matter up with Mr. Godfrey."

What was the reaction of Arthur Godfrey? As might be expected, he ignored the protest and kept right on in his vulgar, vile way. As *Time* reported, "Godfrey's reaction to the matter was as invisible as the chicken in the soup."

The magazine *Glance,* although devoted to advancing the "entertainment" world, raises the question as to whether TV has already gone too far in popularizing obscenity and indecency. This magazine comments: "No medium of entertainment has ever come closer to the American family than television. Each day, receptions are piped directly into millions of homes. To many people, it seems that television has more responsibility toward its audience than radio, or the films. Yet, both radio and movies have censorship codes which seem to grow stricter with the years. So far, television has gotten away literally with murder. Some of the programs are so gruesome that many parents object vigorously. Also, while undressed chorus girls and V-necked charmers are 'visiting' (through TV) bachelor apartments, wives and mothers who also see these shows have raised many a shocked eyebrow. Do you think that television should go unbridled, since it is in its buoyant infancy, or should controls be leveled? Do the wholesome, educational and entertaining features of TV compensate for the sexy, lurid and frightening programs?"

In his article in the Los Angeles *Daily News*, Roy Ringer tells of how his friends kept a "close watch on their sons' favorite television programs." In one week, the "diet" included a total of 67 deaths: "Among them were stabbings, drownings, shootings, strangulation, burial alive, falls from high places, scalpings, poisonings, and disintegration from rays from outer space. And for every death, the boys saw at least two ruthless beatings, bizarre tortures and, particularly, brutality toward women — the latter almost always in a state of undress."

In my book, *Moscow Over Hollywood**, evidence is supplied to show that pro-Communist "thought-control" artists have used the movies as a weapon for the corruption of American youth. Television has been prostituted by Holly-

---

*You may have a copy of this book by sending $1 to help with the Prisoners Bible Broadcast.

wood reds and pinks to accomplish the same purpose. The magazine *Prevue* raises the question: "Is Hollywood on a brutality binge?" It reports, "On Nov. 14, 1953 in a small Ohio town, two 13-year-old boys were brought before authorities for having beaten a 10-year-old badly enough to send him to the hospital. They were re-enacting a movie."

The movies and television seem to operate to make heroes and "great lovers" of male stars who slap, beat, slug and otherwise abuse their girl friends. Kendis Rochlen, columnist for the *Mirror* newspaper, says that the influence of TV and the movies is to cause "gals to coo at the hero who slugs the dame that he kisses." A "new type of lover" has been developed who is "rough and tough" and "cruel."

Students of crime have long known that there is a twisted type of sex pervert who "enjoys" abusing women. His "love-making," if his criminal lust can be called that, always involves some degree of brutality — often ending in murder, in the extreme form. It is claimed that there are some women who are so near to insanity that they "want" to be mistreated. In movie and TV dramas, heroes and "glamorous lovers" are made of abusers of women. "And the gals eat it up," says Kendis Rochlen. This degenerate kind of "entertainment" is bound to turn many boys into brutes and even criminals. The magazine *Night and Day*, which calls itself "America's Picture Magazine of Entertainment," runs an article on the subject, "Should women be manhandled?" It says, "The answer is an unqualified *yes*."

Is it any wonder that assaults on women are among the types of crime that are increasing most rapidly among young Americans?

This article goes on, "Women fall for power in men — any

kind of power. It may be financial, political, or best of all, physical. Watch the faces of women at the fights. They are entranced by the brutality, the cruelty. Their eyes grow dim with passion at the sight of some bruiser with a terrific wallop in either hand. The movie people, experts in mob psychology, are masters in exploiting this quality in women. Hundreds of successful pictures have been based on little more than a magnificent hunk of man cuffing a woman about or otherwise humiliating her. In the Twenties and early Thirties, Jimmy Cagney rose to stardom on the strength of his ability to beat up women with sincerity and conviction. One of the greatest movie scenes of all time was the one in which Cagney jammed a half grapefruit into the face of a pretty girl who had displeased him. The Cagney of today is Marlon Brando, a primitive physical type who overnight became the heart-throb of American women for his brutal treatment of Vivian Leigh in *Streetcar Named Desire*. Dirty, ignorant, talking in coarse grunts, Brando seemed infinitely desirable to most women, as he grabbed Vivian Leigh and violated her."

Television has done much to "popularize" a new kind of "wrestling." The old kind of wrestling, that boys used to engage in at school, involved a fair testing of strength. But the new kind of TV "wrestling" is a contest in "dirtiness," with eye-gouging, kicks in the face, and every kind of foul conduct openly practiced. In fact, the most "popular" wrestlers are those that engage in the most unfair and unsportsmanlike conduct. Some sports writers say that TV wrestling is a "put-up" or "put-on" job and that it is all "fixed" in advance. They say that the wrestlers are not hurt as badly as they pretend to be, although some have to be hospitalized after being "fouled." However, the brutality is all "real" enough to the masses of TV viewers; otherwise, they'd get no "kick" out of it.

At boy scout meetings and Sunday school, boys are taught always to play fair and be kind and gentle. But their "education" via TV consists of making heroes and high-priced stars out of wrestlers who deliberately break all the rules and indulge in every form of dirtiness and unfairness. No wonder that America has a bumper crop of teen-age thugs, ruffians, crooks, brutes, and mobsters who terrorize American community life.

The noted columnist, George Sokolsky, observes, "What with murder a daily fare on TV, the private-eye story being a substitute for the tiresome soap opera and a means to avoid controversy, with many toys imitations of murderous weapons, with comics for children emphasizing murder, it is not surprising that crime is increasingly fashionable and that young boys strut their heroics before boy-crazy teen-agers . . ."

Senator Hendrickson of New Jersey is chairman of the Senate subcommittee studying juvenile delinquency. His committee carefully polled grade school, high school, and college students. Three out of four of the students said there was nothing "wrong about lying and cheating." The Committee found further, "More than 12% of these young people did not consider stealing particularly wrong and 9% would not agree that it is delinquent to rob. Approximately 15% could see no delinquency traits in wanton destruction of property and some 17% shunt aside the venality of sex abuses."

There have been spreading scandals among college athletes who have "sold out to gamblers" and arranged for "fixing" football and basketball games. The pattern is set by TV, which specializes in "wrestling shows" which are openly said to be "fixed" and "faked." The public is fooled and the "performers" or "athletes" get rich by calculated deceit, deliberate "faking," and every form of underhanded trickery.

The TV-movie glorification of violence and crime has produced among young people what the New York Daily News has called "The new three Rs—rowdyism, riot, and revolt." This leading newspaper in America's largest city declares, "A teen-age reign of terror has transformed New York City's public-school system into a vast incubator of crime in which wayward and delinquent youngsters receive years of 'protection' while developing into toughened and experienced criminals." Among school children, there is a "rising rate of rape, assault, knifings, thefts and dope addiction."

Time magazine reports, March 15, 1954, "Some time after-hours last week, a band of vandals broke into Manhattan's Junior High School for a lively round of delinquents' sport. They plugged up a sink on the top floor, turned on the faucets and let a flood of water spread throughout the building. They invaded a science classroom, smashed its vials, overturned desks, scattered papers and exhibits over the floor. They sprayed halls and corridors with fire extinguishers, partly burned a school banner, slashed furniture in a teachers' lounge, spattered paint through two classrooms, tore up books in the library." *Time* comments, "But to veteran Manhattan teachers, all this was not unusual. In the past few years, they have became increasingly accustomed to it."

The magazine continues, "In some New York schools, teachers estimate that fully half the pupils carry pushbutton switch-blade knives or homemade zipguns. Many of these guns are made in the school machine shops . . . Many students have devised ingenious flame throwers, and others carry plastic water pistols loaded with searing or blinding chemical solutions . . . Kids threaten and have beaten up teachers who wouldn't graduate or promote them . . . In Brooklyn, a teacher who reported a group of vandals to the principal was confronted in his office the next day and told he would be thrown out the window the next time he 'snitched.' In one school, a teacher recently stopped a fight between two students. Later that day, he found his new car scratched and marked up by one of the boys . . . Last year a student roughed up a male teacher without being disciplined. Another student struck a woman teacher . . . At Jamaica High School in Queens, a teacher challenged three teen-age intruders in the corridors. They turned on him savagely and cut him with their fists . . . At Frederick Douglass Junior High School an instructor was asked why the corridors and classrooms were scrawled with numerous variations of a single obscene theme. The tecaher winced, but replied wryly, 'Oh—ah—it's sort of a school motto here."

It is hard to believe that any medium of so-called "entertainment" could sink lower than the movies. But TV has hit a new "bottom" of degradation. Consider the case of the well-known actress, Martha Scott. In movies, she had been starred as "a noble, sacrificial" type of girl. But TV made a murderess out of her, and Miss Scott claims she likes the criminal role much better. In his syndicated column, Erskine Johnson says, "Martha Scott loves to kill brother, poison husband" (in the telecast, of course). Miss Scott says that TV took off the "shackles": "I was always typed in Hollywood as a noble dame . . . But TV has given me murder and even glamor."

TV surveys put the Godfrey show in number two position,

from the popularity standpoint. Most "popular" program, seen by more millions of TV viewers than any other, is said to be the "I Love Lucy" show. In third place place is the Jackie Gleason show which, as Mr. Rayburn reports, features this "fat and untidy" person "planting a long and passionate kiss on his seductive television wife, then leeringly wiping his mouth off afterward as the camera came in for a close-up."

Revelation tells us that there will be a world-wide audience to gaze upon the two murdered martyrs, left unburied in the street. Perhaps, as a warm-up for this hellish spectacle, the "I Love Lucy" show created a "sensation" by presenting Lucille Ball in all stages of pregnancy. As Mr. Rayburn comments, "For weeks we had Lucy and her husband making all sorts of jokes about being pregnant on the 'I Love Lucy' show." As one newspaper observer said, "It was anything for a laugh —and I mean *anything*. The expectant mother and her devoted husband had a great time showing her off, 'big as a barrel' and 'clumsy as a cow,' as a friendly commentator affectionately put it. We don't have to ask the question, anymore: is nothing sacred? So far as TV is concerned, the answer is *no*. With approaching motherhood made into a vulgar spectacle and object of nasty jokes, we must face the fact: everything is subject to commercialization on TV."

What company undertook to "exploit" pregnancy, and make money out of displaying it in all its stages? Why, the Philip Morris Cigaret Co., of course. Every doctor will tell you, if he is honest and not bought off by the cigaret trust, that the worst thing for an expectant mother is nicotine. Dr. Walter Wilson, the famous Kansas City physician, says that cigaret-smoking is the greatest single cause of miscarriage. I do not know if Lucille Ball actually smokes, or just gives the impression that she is a Philip Morris addict. But the whole effect of her "show" was to create a tie-up between cigarets and motherhood. Cigaret-smoking and motherhood are supposed to go together!

The magazine *TV and Movie Screen* has an article on Lucy and her husband. It says, "When Philip Morris became interested in Desi's idea for 'I Love Lucy' and the pilot film had to be made, Lucy discovered that she was pregnant. She had to decide whether to wait to make the pilot film after the baby was born and so perhaps lose the chance of a sponsor or go ahead with the movie and risk losing the baby. It was not an easy choice for Lucille and Desi, who had lost one child while they were touring with their act."

All Christian parents must feel very sorry for this poor woman, who, through moral weakness, and love of money, let her unborn baby be made a TV spectacle, as one commentator said, "like a two-headed calf in the sideshow of the circus."

Readers Digest, May, 1954, has an article on *The Real Story of Lucille Ball*. Here the whole sordid story is told of how Mrs. Arnaz's pregnancy was seized upon as a "gimmick" to be exploited, for the profit of the cigaret company, on TV. Lucy and Desi were just getting started on TV, we are told: "Then came bombshell news: Lucille was pregnant again. Delighted but wryly aware of the fact that she would be pregnant during the whole fall season, Lucille telephoned her TV producer, Jesse Oppenheimer, expecting a flood of pessimism. Instead, Oppenheimer made a remark that is now famous in show business. 'Boy whatta gimmick!' he chortled. 'In the show we'll have Lucy Ricardo pregnant, too.' "

There are a number of popular TV shows which pretend to portray "family life." Many TV viewers, perhaps have not detected the poison hidden in these allegedly "humorously innocent" dramas. Barry Nelson is the "lesser half" in the popular TV show entitled *My Favorite Husband*. Mr. Nelson protests, "Why must all husbands in television situation comedies be boobs, the butt of countless practical jokes and generally possessing the intelligence of a four-year-old child? Hardly a night goes by that some poor sucker doesn't get himself into a nonsensical situation on TV that no ordinary self-respecting American husband would find himself in."

Instead of teaching children to honor and respect their fathers, the influence of TV is to make the supposed "head of the house" into a fool in the sight of his wife and children. Mr. Nelson truly says, "Youngsters are getting the wrong impression of their fathers and grown-up males in general, just by watching these TV shows." Our juvenile courts are congested with youthful wrongdoers who have been taught by TV to sneer at their fathers, their fathers' faith and Bible. The typical TV "family entertainment program" presents the teen-age boy or girl as constantly correcting stupid parents. The "humor" of the situation is supposedly supplied when it is shown that the teen-ager "knew best" and that father was just a blundering simpleton in trying to impose his ideas upon his children.

Much of what passes as TV humor could scarcely be "enjoyed" by anyone with even a smattering of Christian conscience. A survey showed that these are the main "themes" of TV humor:

The antics of drunks.

The gutter-level double-meaning "jokes" of Godfrey & Co.

The "homosexual motif," in which some TV comedian

lisps or swings his hips like the "fairies" and "queers" are supposed to do.

The "family comedy situation" in which, no matter what he says or does, father is made to be an idiot in the sight of his wife and children.

We have pointed out how the movies and television make male "heroes" of characters who play parts featuring brutality and sex perversion. Now let us take a look at the "heroines" of the TV screen. The magazine *Tempo* has an article on what it calls, "The Cult of Wicked Women." It says that the Hollywood controllers of movies and TV are "convinced that good girls are dull girls." Therefore, heroines are made out of characters who show the worst degrees of wickedness.

This magazine declares, "Today's heroines were educated in the gutter." It gives some examples. Eartha Kitt made a big name for herself in show business by signing the theme-song: "I wanna be evil." Nightclub and TV star, Lilly Christine, boasts, "The more vicious I look, the more men pant." Marilyn Monroe is quoted as saying, "Men have always liked the idea of being ruined by a wicked woman—if she's pretty."

From the beginning, TV was seized upon by the cigaret and beer and wine companies and ever since it has been exploited to turn more Americans into nicotine and alcohol addicts. Although cigaret-smoking is the greatest of menaces to both mothers and babies, we have seen how a cigaret company tied-in motherhood with the use of its poisonous product. Every athlete and every high school athletic coach knows that alcoholic beverage is a destroyer of healthy manhood. Yet, the major boxing bouts, as well as other athletic contests, are "sponsored" on TV by the beer companies. Big-name baseball stars are quoted on TV as recommending cigarets, although all baseball players, like all doctors, know that smoking is harmful, and any recommendation they make is just for a fat fee.

The American Cancer Society made the most careful study of the effects of cigaret-smoking. It filed its report with the American Medical Association in San Francisco. This is what was proved, according to the *United States News and World Report:*

The "death rate" from all causes is 75% higher among heavy smokers than among non-smokers. Death from heart disease is 95% higher among heavy smokers than among non-smokers. Death from all forms of cancer is 156% higher among smokers than non-smokers. Death from lung cancer is 400% higher among smokers than non-smokers.

But TV is largely "sold out" to the cigaret profiteers, who use millions of dollars of advertising space on the TV screens to spread lying propaganda in favor of cigaret-smoking. So long as it is so largely controlled by the cigaret trust, television will function as a menace to the health and morals of our people. Truth itself is murdered on the TV screen by those who make profits out of luring and deluding our people into forming and maintaining the cancer-causing, killing "cigaret habit."

TV advertising has been prostituted to the ultimate lengths in presenting beer and wine drinking as "healthful," "relaxing," "desirable" and "part of the American way of life." TV has doubtless been the largest single factor in contributing to the appalling increase of drinking among teen-agers. "Ninety percent of high school students drink alcoholic beverages," according to a survey of Nassau County, New York. The corruption of the home, through the horrible example set on

TV programs, is apparently one of the main causes of youthful drinking. The poll, as reported in *Better Homes and Gardens* magazine, shows that about 75% of the teen-age drinkers "took their first drinks" at home with parental consent. Seventeen percent of the youths questioned said that they "began drinking before the age of 11." At the age of 14, 79% were drinking "occasionally" and at the age of 16, 90% were drinking "regularly."

Dr. Fredrich Wertham, in his *Seduction of the Innocent,* offers a very complete analysis of the influence of television upon young people. He reports, "About one third of all television programs for children have to do with crime or violence. . . . The brutality in TV crime shows is so insidiously glorified that many people do not recognize it as such any more and accept it as smart . . . Murders, gunshots and violent acts are as plentiful on TV as raisins in a raisin cake—in fact, some producers seem to think they *are* the raisins. An average child who is no particular television addict and takes what is offered absorbs from five to eleven murders a day from television."

Dr. Wertham goes on, "A cartoon in *Pathfinder* magazine with a woman sitting before a television screen saying, 'This one had a happy ending—she finally murders her husband . . .' is no just a joke. In a serious vein, the television version of *Macbeth* with the head cut off on stage and later shown in close-up is typical of the crudity of style and cruelty of content."

The Doctor tells of interviewing a delinquent boy who said, "I spend about six hours a day on television."

"What happens?" he was asked.

"People get murdered. People kill for money, for property

or for power. They kill women because they are going to tell on them or something. It may be the girl friend of the murderer or a cook that may be murdered. Sometimes the girls do the killing. They shoot them. There is one program where the man needed pills, he had a bad heart. The girl took the pills out of his reach, and moved his phone so he couldn't call anybody, and his pen and pencil so he couldn't write anything, then he died. She was married to him. She killed him because she was tired of him. (This was related in a matter-of-fact way, as if describing a self-understood circumstance)."

Dr. Wertham continues, "About seven months later this boy was arrested for stealing. I examined him again and closed my report to the Children's Court with these words: This is a typical case of a boy who has spent many hours a day looking at television programs, many of which glorify crime, violence, lawlessness, and depict these scenes in emotionally alluring detail. Under these circumstances, it seems to me not surprising that a boy succumbs to temptation and I believe that the adult world is more to be blamed than this individual child, who has made a good effort to adjust himself. I should point out to the Court that the observations of the bad effect of television programs on this boy were recorded on the chart several months before he was arrested for these delinquencies."

Dr. Wertham speaks of "television's immense potentialities." He says, "Television is on the way to become the greatest medium of our time." Because television brings the degenerate dance hall, the saloon, the brothel, what amounts to a near-nudist colony, right into the living rooms of millions of homes, it wields a power for evil greater even than the motion picture theater.

The same evil forces that took hold of Hollywood and spread degeneracy through the movies, have now seized upon the even more potent propaganda force of television. To a large degree, these same pagan powers have taken over the writing of high school textbooks and the shaping of our American educational system.

People interested in pursuing this subject further might benefit from securing my book on *Moscow Over Hollywood*. This book shows how a dictatorship over the thought and life of America has been projected from Moscow through the utilization of clever and cunning propaganda. I will be glad to send the book to anyone asking for it, when mailing in an offering of $1 or more for the Prisoners Bible Broadcast.

In this book, I have sought to present the truth about TV. Is it television — or hellevision? Make up your own mind. Draw your own conclusion — on the basis of the evidence.

Knowing the evil that encompasses American youth, let us all pray for the young people of our land. Let us pray for a revival of righteousness in America. Let us pray: Come quickly, Lord Jesus.

In Christ is our hope and deliverance. Let us trust in Him. Let us look to Him in this time of great national peril, and great spiritual need.